leaves
of
love

Remnants of a Romantic

Christopher Oak Reinier

For my children, Jill, Jason, Kynd, and Ya,
who have blessed me with the strong, imaginative, self-sufficient,
loving ways they have chosen their admirable partners — Mike,
Catherine, Dave, and Gabriel — lived their lives, and launched six
fine children into this world:
Nataniel, LeeAnn, Joshua, Dylan, Sierra, and Oscar,

and for my lovely wife, Darcy,
her sons, Tom and Joe, their wives, Tracy and Jessica,
and Tom and Tracy's newborn, Ethan,

all of them graceful in their meetings with the challenges and
treats of love.

With special thanks to poets Carol Lundberg, Mike Tuggle, and
Sandy Eastoak for their writing and inspiration, and to my editor,
Harker Brautighan, for her excellent help.

Contents

Dedication – 1
In the Morning Sunlight – 2
A Leaf of Love – 3
Elixir – 4
Elementary Love – 6
Out of the Wilds – 8
Dairy Cream Doggerel – 9
The Kiss – 11
Saving It for Marriage, 1950s – 12
Freed – 13
Innocence – 14
Your Lips – 15
She lying naked – 16
The Velvet Fox – 17
Chimera – 18
To Begin Again – 20
Katy Did – 21
From Your Shoulder – 22
Grace – 23
Time out of Time – 24
Woman – 25
Last Love Poem – 26
Deer Heart – 27
How It Changes – 28
When We Walk – 30
Thanks Be to You – 31
And There Is Marriage – 32
Family Cloth – 33
Marriage, a Poem – 34
The Chasm – 35
Spilled – 36
Other End of Eden – 37
They Will Come at You – 38
Autumn Moon – 39

My Child – 41
His Hands – 42
Nightmare – 44
How Could I? – 46
When I Fall in Love – 47
Love Is – 49
Father of the West – 50
The Keeper – 52
Ode to My Wallet – 54
In the Turning of Leaves – 56
Lost in the Woods – 57
Finding Today – 58
Old Friends – 63
Waiting – 64
River Flowing Far Beyond – 65

The poems in this book move from youth to old age as
leaves might unfold, mature, ripen, and fall.

The poems, "Grace", "From Your Shoulder" and "Katy Did"
were previously published on-line in
The Red Wolf Journal, "Seeing Beauty" Winter 2015/2016.

**Dedicated
to:**

the living
the freeing
the true-speaking ones

the giving
the seeing
the job-doing ones

the gentle
the playful
the brave, humble ones

the peaceful
the careful
the daring in love

and to:

the mothers
the fathers
the children everywhere

the sisters
the brothers
the strangers who care

the old friends
the new friends
the life that we share

the fire
the water
the earth and the air.

1

In the Morning Sunlight

droplets of diamonds adorn
the needles of the
rain-soaked redwood trees –

glints of sapphires,
garnets, emeralds –

a glistening wealth of jewels.

I'll take them all, thank you,
at least as many as I can see,
stash them in the top drawer
of my memory,

there,
where I keep the county carnival lights,
the waves at Blind Beach,
my mother's smile.

A Leaf of Love

The times she loved me
were moments
cast upon a wishing stream –

one today,
another next year,
another might have been
a dream...

She had so many other children.

But a leaf of love could
float and twirl and keep me
playing there.

The years flowed on
as deep moving water

into which I plunged and
almost drowned, reaching
for the safety of a leaf.

Elixir

As if I had put my nose to a potpourri
of flowers, leaves, perfumes, spices
that touched my life with ambrosia,

or wandered past a table full of memories
that more than nourished me,
seasoned as they were with ecstasy,

a certain aroma sends me back
to that childhood feeling of well-being.

Throughout the years
I must have searched for it,
as one who tries to re-inhabit a dream,
and thought I found it in:

the tadpole hopeful air of Spring, fresh with song
  in my Midwest blackbird heaven;

the wafting smells of the cuisine teasing me
  from doorways in Times Square,1957;

the balm of curry coming from the kitchen of
  the one with yellow eyes and what I went to find;

the smell of well-aged comfort in a living room
  warm and softly lit, where everything is handy;

the evening incense swirling through my mind
  dark curtains promising exotic things behind;

the amber promise of relaxation in the breath
  and silky bite from a snifter of dry brandy;

the wisps of smoke from burning leaves
  sweet scented from an autumn long ago;

or even in that cold clear deliverance
   of a walk in freshest snow…

But, no,

after all, and first of all…
it was that waking smell,

adults were up already
talking over coffee,
a lilting conversation,
their early morning voices
careful of the place.

And we were children waking
to the smell of frying bacon.

Elementary Love

In the first grade,
Sally had Shirley-Temple curls,
and she lifted up her dress
to show me her panties.

In the second grade,
when I tried to kiss her,
Sally told the teacher.

In the third grade,
the three girls who sat behind me
sent me little notes that said:
"Will you fuck me?"
and I wrote back, "Yes,"
but I never had to do it.

In the fourth grade,
we played Horse and Rider.
The girls got on the boys' shoulders,
then they tried to push each other off,
squeezing and wiggling against our necks.

In the fifth grade,
I was in love with the teacher's daughter,
but she went to another school,
and I almost never saw her.
She only came with us on field trips,
and when she did I sat beside her.

In the sixth grade,
I just wanted to play
baseball and soccer.

In the seventh grade,
Richard and Johnny and I got boners
(and they weren't about the stupid girls;
boners just happened).
We didn't know what to do with them:
how not to have them show.
Should they go up towards the belt
or down the legs below?

In the eighth grade,
some of my classmates
went with Maria
into the high-grass field,
and they said they did it with her.

I wanted to do it with her too, but I
sat alone in the woods by the creek,
getting hot from watching water spiders mate,
or turned on watching rutting dogs in heat
when warm spring days made my
wanting ache.

Out of the Wilds

When I was nine
and she was eight
in the woods
on the leafy floor

she let me,
maybe giggling,
I don't remember.

Afterwards, the looks –
not from a fearsome god –
more from the silence,
as everything is known,
even by the dog
and the bird in the tree.

On the school bus,
she almost told
her girlfriends,
who, by their faces,
forewarned her.

After all,
we could not talk about it,
not even to each other.

Out of the wilds we grew,
learning to survive,
and to build the silence
that fences in
the cultivated gardens of our lives.

Dairy Cream Doggerel

George, he was a very good man,
captain of the football team.
Chuck, he came from Alabam –
or was it Mississip-pie-eee?
We were high school buddies then,
called ourselves "The Be-eeg Three".
But we weren't more than any of them
who got their kicks at the Dairy Queen.

Chuck was a hustler, a pool shark.
He had the girls; he had the dare,
an all-American football star,
so pretty he made the girls swear.
'Course, all we wanted was to have a car,
a car to take, with well-groomed hair,
up to the drive-in beneath the stars.
O Dairy Queen Baby, come over here!

Chuck was a fox and smooth as the moon,
made life seem easy like he didn't care.
He could drawl like a dripping spoon
filled with honey from the County Fair.
George had ducktails just like Elvis,
strong like an ox, grace like a deer.
He knew how to swing his pelvis,
but he was shy as a baby steer.

I was a corn-pone country-boy loon,
'bout as sexy as a straight-backed chair,
just kept singing the same old tune,
O Dairy Queen Baby, come over here!

While we three planned which girl we'd kiss,
with no idea what we had to fear,
we mumbled and stuttered like big dumb-wits
when that Dairy Queen Baby came over here!

We in the car knew every tune,
listened, licked ice cream, and had to stare.
Ask her, please, "How High the Moon?"
hatched our plots to keep her there,
sweet teen angel in the fantasies
of three boys sitting with well-groomed hair,
themselves not more than vagaries
in their Dairy Queen Baby young dreamy affair.

The Kiss

It got Rosie
and it got me

at the movies
when we were fourteen –

lights flickering on her face,
pink perfume wafting
across the space
between her cheek
and mine,
causing an ache
the only cure for which
was a suicidal leap –

I landed on her lips,
which also seemed
to land on mine!
O!
the softness of the heat!

Yes, I kissed Rosie!
And she kissed me!
Wait until I tell somebody!

Saving It for Marriage, 1950s
(Or Blue Balls of Spring)

Oh swingingly breaking,
Love her and aching!
Prom Queen and Ellington,
kiss, touch and feel um −

Oh my my! Oh no no!
Save it for marriage! Oh!
Hot nineteen-fifties,
wet dreams and nifties,
down we will not! Oh no no!

Walk home and hurt, oh
moon, oh, and gleaming,
sexual dreaming,
Victorian angel,
groin aching hell! Oh!

Swingingly breaking,
love her and aching!

Freed

The heart of life so loved,
grown so big,
the hurt, the anger
discarded, let go,
the hard scarred skin of a childhood
formed in a hostile world
fallen away and left behind.

Could it be true?
be different? be new?

Now she could feel the warmth,
the sun on her wings,
and she knew she was going to fly.

Innocence

Sitting on the bed,
we drank a cup of hot chocolate
with a marshmallow floating
sweet on top of it.

The cup emptied,
we placed it by the bed,
and fell asleep
in love
at peace
in the night
with the moon floating
sweet on top of it.

Your lips

I keep seeing
your delicate lips

      against the glass of fine red wine

your mouth
      as you speak
      exquisitely tweaked

      immortalized
      in a painting of

           a subtly
           injured beauty

I keep seeing your

      remarkable face

your mouth

      how it should be kissed…

She lying naked

here beside me
(except for her black shoes)

her leg
thigh

flower-petal skin

her knee cap
a sea shell
beneath her silky sand

I wiggle it.

Her calf
firm in my hand

her shoes
open at the toes
black straps around her ankles

her toes
tickle tickle between her toes
tickle tickle

and while she giggles

quickly up to kiss her mouth
her eyes
her cheek
the jasmine by her ear
and to bury my face in her blooming hair.

The Velvet Fox

Has amber eyes
(I know because
I looked.)

> She has a secret corner
> in her smile.

She runs across me with her soft paws,
and licks me with her velvet tongue.

It will make me laugh when I wake up.

I do,

and I try to catch her tail as she bounds away.

Chimera

I see her.
She sees me.

I follow her,
      the gliding way she moves
      between the open fields
      and the shadows of the trees.

She turns to tease me on,
      humming flowing promises,
      lilting in the moonlight,
      hips waving like the
      seas rise and fall on softest sand.

I lose her in the moon.

She peeks from a cloud,
      is a changing shape,
      a night-bird, a nymph,
      a silver moth,
      mother of the seasons,
      eons of plans instinctively hers,
      unspokenly whole.

And she leads me on
      to the cave of spider light,
      smell of urine at the opening,
      others from another storyline
      unknown to me
      have come and gone,
      marking time.

She takes me in,
      and with a mournful piercing tongue
      sings me wondrous lies,
      one verse so sad and then another,
      music etched onto my mind.

I reach to her my softest hands,
draw from her what has the sound of pain.

I take her in my arms –

       then all sparks!
       quick lightnings!
       turnings and rhythms,
       wild and rolling
       in tumultuous waves
       washed to the sea,

she lifts me and drops me
       on a star-darkened beach,
       and is gone like the tide,

not even goodbye.

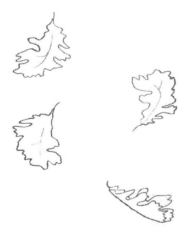

19

To Begin Again

Late at night, I sit,
my aching soul flown away,
fluttering around my memory of you,
not you, my memory of you,

a distant flame,
flickering, burning here, then there.

Come back, I call to my soul,
come back from yearnings,
from flutterings,
from would-be flights...

Come back and be the one
my caterpillar needs
to weave its hard and dark cocoon.

Katy Did

Katy did,
and Katy does,
and, yes, I like her way.
What she did she does with love.
That's all I need to say.

But I'd say more,
if words could carry dynamite,
if ways of speaking were like laughing music,
if grace come walking quickly from a distance
could be described: light, swift, certain, wild –

a shadow in the corner of my eye,
bursting into starlight,
and smiling all the way.

Oh heart!
How many strikings can you stay?

From Your Shoulder

Yes,
I do
love to
touch and
lightly trace
the subtle slope
from your shoulder
down to your breast,
the way your skin lies,
like silk laid softly down
from the shoulder of a great
and graceful mountain - the very
mountain whose grace can best be
understood by knowing this about
you: this sweet slope from your
shoulder to your breast. For
only by knowing this can one
know how grand yet lovely
soft and fragile can be
the shoulder of a
mountain.

Grace

There is in the grace
of your woman-ness,
in your voice,
a light caress, yes,
in your body's word,
a lilt, not consciously
addressing –

but quietly,
a simple gesture,

a small gift –
like a swallow
flying lightly on a breeze,
needing only the arc
of its flight.

Time out of Time

Beyond was
the music of padding feet
the standings of laughter
wailings of ancient songs

snow on the mountain
valleys of olive
thickets of orchids.

We took the
privilege of illusion
drugged by love
afloat in a
perfect confluence
of bodies of skin
of lips of eyes
of knowing

Yes,
there is blood
in this knowing,
unto death
in this having —

her face like the sun,
her body the earth
in all its solid colors —

with her,
she who would have
given birth to us

could we have
made it
back
in to time.

Woman

Heart of your own
here with me

We touch
and
I believe your kiss
and
I believe your breath
and
I believe the earth and the sky
and
your shoulders and your eyes
and
the water and the fire
and
your belly and your warmth
warmth and desire
and

I hear your heart
the ancient rhythm
beating for the
moment moment

and with
the kiss of lust and love
the fire, the water, the earth,

I take you
I enter you

and
I give myself to you
woman
oh woman!

Last Love Poem

Let's build a home.
That's what I want to do.
The muse will have to forgive it.
I wanted to write a love poem.
But the way I feel about you,
I'd rather live it.

Deer Heart

On our wedding night,
a friend brought a deer,
a yearling,
he had hit with his car
on the road to our cabin.

Skinned,
there was meat
on the shoulders
and on the hips,
not much else.

We found the liver
and the little heart,
little blue heart.
I fried it and
ate it and
it melted in my mouth.

When I went to bed,
she stayed up late talking
with our friend who brought the deer.

I remember best now
the little blue heart.

How it Changes

She was a wild and sassy thing,
flicking her tail, clicking her hoofs,
free to leap from cliff to cliff,
and when the lion came
she flew with the eagles.

All dancing she could be,
all playful rock to rock,
and foraging around the mountain side,
she was the sun, the moon, the clouds, the rain,
the distant river running down the valley floor,
she a moving part of it,
flowing from the sunlight to the moonlit ridge,
bounding up the crevice to the high stone ledge.
Oh free she was!

And when you descended
out of your high-ground stomping camp,
when you strutted the ground,
came to her, rose over her,
and thrust into her wanting you,
Oh! free she was! and of immortal sound!

Now began her filling,
her slowing, and her lying down,
her cramping, churning,
grunting, pressing, spreading,
holding on, letting go,
the slipping-out relief,
the licking, licking, nuzzling, nursing,
on the holding ground.

But soon
the lurking of the lion!
And the little wobbly
babe between her legs…

She is a different one,
become the mother,
become another.

Time for you?
Well, some, but…
you'll need to earn it.

When We Walk

So smooth and warm the evening air,
as I take your hand on the road through the woods,
the air that soothes my face as I walk beside you here —

along where the four-leaf clovers hide until
you find them in the clustered sorrel and
take them home to dry.

A towhee cheeps in a tree nearby.
Could it be the one we feed?
A wishful kinship with the wild.

We pass the spring-filled water tank,
stop and listen to the water like
liquid silver from the forest's bank.

We're not rich, but I have all I need,
food at home in the pantry, the water…
the forest's welcoming sigh,
and you are next to me.

Thanks Be to You

The touch of your hand on my arm
Your bright unassuming charm
The way you kneel by the fire
How you make me laugh with your fine one-liners
Your smile when you open the door
Your genius for making the TV work

Your steady swinging thumping bass guitar
Your focus on the placement of the coaster
Your thoughtful selfless generosity
The way you show me what I need to see
How you respond to others' needs with perfect timing
At ease with life's so careless and imperfect rhyming

The purity of your voice when you are singing
Your easy good-sport way of doing almost anything
The way you stack the cups and pans and everything
Your quiet courage when you are hurting
Your gentle playful way of making love
Your lasagna, frittata, and perfect bacon

Your savvy comments on the morning news
Your choice of socks, blacks or dark blues
The easy unselfconscious way you get dressed
The effortless way you take care of business
How you make for us a loving space
Your loveliness and beautiful face

All these years you've given me you
Darcy Louise, I do love you.

And There Is Marriage

There is the caress of the courtesan, the romance of the duke,
the thrill of a shooting star, the love of a cresting wave,
the single blossom of a sacred lily.

One can live a life of hide and seek in the woods, in the crowds,
in oneself, find inscrutable ways of dressing, if seen at all,
the naked truth...

And there is marriage:

> a delicate thing,
> fragily connecting
> two people with
> the gravity that holds the
> planets in their orbits,
> the molten mass
> at the center of the earth,
>
> their new roots, the
> filaments of life, moving
> deeper in the dark,
> their connection begat
> from lust and love,
> rights and wrongs
> peace and war,
>
> traveling together —
>
>> without moving,
>> inside the infinite circle of life and death,
>> across the diameter, across that path from
>> one side of the circle to the other, that long,
>> pointless path, marking along the way
>> memories to which they return together —
>
> holding hands.

Family Cloth

They
have come.
They have gone.
We had ocean-beach,
hanging-out, family-sewing fun.

Carefully choosing yarns and colors,
we told more of our stories, stitched more
threads between the fabrics of our lives.

Mothers, fathers, children, uncles, aunts
talked and fussed and laughed beneath the moon,

then lay down to sleep together in the cluttered rooms,
our love like a hand-sewn quilt, not perfectly done,
but warm and lying lightly over us.

Marriage, a Poem

Poets have not been good to marriage
Check it out to see how much 'tis so
Wendell Barry aside, it's a subject
Muttered as a sour kind of woe
Not very often with a passion and a glow

marriage can get long for the poetic word

It scruffs along the unsung, the unspoken
The fluffing of the other's pillow
The coffee bringing, dishes doing
Band-aid putting, listening extra slow
Keeping things okay, and through the valley below

but if you've made it together with the truth of it

The pleasure you have in sharing nothing to do
The giving back of what you had to borrow
A mumbly-dumb candle light dinner together
The kids, the grandkids, an acceptance of sorrow
A river of muddy times and plans for tomorrow

and the truth is whether you did it or didn't

Made the swim together in the great ocean's tides
Felt the swell and the dip, the rip and the flow
Fixed the boat in the storm, pulled a child from the deep
Paid the elders their due, helped an apple tree grow
Kept your hearts together when Hell's hammer did blow

gnarled and graced by the force of familiarity

Then sat on the porch at sunset
Or up on the ridge at the end of the road
Or by the river in the evening air
So intimate has been your sharing the load
Yours is the poem of marriage not really meant to be told.

The Chasm

Some thing
happens
to a love:

little
irritations,
minor criticisms,
and it sounds weak
to be hurt so easily,
forget it, never mind, it's
only raindrops, not a storm…

Yet all the little raindrops have soaked the edges
of that place on which we stood together.

Our footholds have
crumbled down,
become a gully running full   of "never minds"
eroded further by a stream of   unexpressed resentments,
cutting out a canyon where   unspoken curses echo from its walls,
a thousand little unvoiced   angers become a deep and silent canyon
cutting through our love,

and

now we stand here   looking at each other
from different distant sides   and memories grow fainter
of when the chasm was   not here. But here it is.
How can it be bridged?   Or will we, already so alone,
will we turn and   go our separate ways,
all those little raindrops   compounded now into a river
muddied with the ground   where we once stood
together   in love?

Spilled

I look
at myself:

strong bodied,
but powerless,

brain working
well enough
to know
I've failed in love,

broken your trust,
as simply as one tips
and breaks a glass
while reaching for the bottle,

the love I had for you,
splashed across the floor,

and you are gone.

I can clean it up,
and will,
but you will still be hurt,
and the glass

shattered.

Other End of Eden

I wish I could have begun this as a happy story,
begun in happiness because it ended in happiness,
a jewel of love for you to wear.
Behold this real thing!
It is possible!

I should have begun it yesterday.

But, as the world does crumble around us,
stinking of foul odors,
as the monster whips its clumsy tail,
struggling against the stupor of approaching extinction,

would it not have been something fine
to have lived a love
that shines out through the gloom,
wondrous as two people,
standing together,
quiet and unafraid,
at the other end of Eden?

They Will Come at You

They will come at you with smiles
Might have tears in their eyes
They will come at you with love
Might tell you clever lies

They will come at you with guns
Might just be holding knives
They will come at you with fists
Might grind yours into grime

You will have asked for it
Invading as you have
The sacred secret circle
Of their married lives.

Autumn Moon

Dead cars by the road,
black butterflies soaring
(vultures romanticized),
dry wind blowing,
turtle drums,
Coltrane on the radio,
down Highway One
after the harvest,
after the fun –

alone.

Stop at Goat Rock,
misty cliffs down
to the calling sea,
the flame of the sun
extinguishing itself on
the table of the ocean
like a candle flaring out.

Watched by giant rocks – the
silhouettes of ancient women,
waves splashing at their skirts –
children scream playfully
in the sundown wind,
then are gone.

Lupine blossoms
stay open to the night
and the light of the moon
rising behind the eastern hills.

I build a little fire
on a sandy dune,
red wine in the bottle,

fire leaping smoke at me.

A time when the growth runs down,
a love is lost, the fire burns out,
and the moon moves across the sky,
a lantern in the dark hand of tomorrow.

My Child

I watch
the clouds
float across your face −

the little red boat
awash awhile
and then your smile

You grow,
and in your raw feast of life
I find my sustenance.

In your laughter
my life is saved.

I have had to go away,
had to leave you.

Yet all my seasons
will turn through you −

my spring in your bright greetings
my summer in your growing
my autumn in your goodbyes
my winter in your absence −

O my child

His Hands

He sits
with his hands
on his knees,
the fire keeping him warm,
rain dripping from the trees.

Your daddy's gone a-hunting,
a-hunting for the word,
but we know the word is "love",
don't we, my baby dear,
we know the word is love,
and it is here.

Cleft from his children
he travels on a
thin arc of madness,
a visceral amber color,
sounding silent but loud,
streaming out and out −
like a ribbon untied −
into the dark

Blow the bubble bye! bye!
Run the race O fly high!
Shoot the basket, try, try...

Sitting in the back seat
licking on an ice-cream treat,

laughing talking getting right,
he takes them home and says
goodnight, his smiling heart squeezed shrieking
tight, the sagging sigh,
the tangled breeze fells him

down to his knees,
wrong! wrong! snapping in his mind.

Must rise…
He knows he must –

> to help them make a
> whole cloth from the tatters,
> balance all the colors,
> learn how to know
> and hold their own,
> wear all of it out with
> good work, big play,
> dance and song,
> and hearts kept strong –

for what he wants,
what he needs of life,
only their happiness
has big enough hands.

Nightmare

I wander through a meadow.
I am strong and lean and free.
I pick a stalk of grain,
put it between my lips.
The sun is warm on my face.

But look! high on that cliff,
wearing her lavender dress.
No, not sunshine, that is her hair.
She calls, "Daddy!" do you hear?
"Daddy, Daddy, catch me, catch me!"
But I am not there…

I walk quickly to nowhere,
my hand at my side,
as it was in hers,
when she skipped with me
to the store.

It is night.
The air is dark and clear.
I sit beside a tree trunk.
Five maidens dance around my fire.
They come to me in turn,
sitting, kneeling, rocking, rolling,
laughing, screaming...

The dream-walls tip and spill.
I stand on a river bank.
Black algae hangs from my shoulders.
Black riverweed drops from my hands.
My baby boy lies on the bed of my arms.
I beg him! I beg him! I beg him!
Wake up my gentle young boy!
Slack is his strong little body.
In my arms he floats home…

Ah! Ah! Ah!
The snowflakes are crystals of blood.
My eyes freeze in their sockets.
My flesh flakes off like bits of ice,

as I bend,
        bend,
            bend…
My hair is shaggy.
My fingernails are black with dirt.
My chin is rough with stubbly hair.
I wear my large work shoes.
I step into my daughter's doll house.
I walk in my daughter's doll house.
I crush beneath my feet a tiny table
and a little chair. I hear the sound.
I do not move.
"Be careful, Daddy," she calls to me.
And I try to step with care,
and I crush a dresser
and a dainty mirror
and my little girl cries,
"Daddy, Daddy!" she cries,
"Daddy, Daddy!"

I wake up.

I listen.

I hear the peaceful
breathing of their sleep.
They are all right!
They are all right!

And I do not have to
take them "home"
until tomorrow night.

How Could I?

Your question cloudy on my mind –
"How could you leave us?
Just walk away?"

I want to run from it and let the rain weep tears for me.
How could I leave you, your childhood need for me
my only certain cause for being?

I told myself, O I reported to the Gods: It was to save us all –
from conflicts come between me and your mother,
neither of us being wrong, but that not making right.

I was no king, who with a cool eye arranges things.
I thought my love for you would grow in ground too cynical,
like poisoned fruit unable to sustain you.

Although you've known me as a man sometimes beside you
or from a distance standing by, I did not realize enough,
before I left, the moments you might miss my heart, my touch,

my being daily there (the way, courageously, your mother's been).
I did not realize how much I'd leave myself when I left you,
always a gaping hole in the center of what happiness I found.

Now you've grown up rich in hope and strong in love,
and maybe there was something right in what has felt so wrong,
even though, if that be so, it's not a truth which fills

the space we did not share – the empty door, the empty chair.
And we go on now
sometimes bumping up against that emptiness.

But when we do,
reaching to each other,
touching, we leave it there.

When I Fall in Love...

It was 1957, Elvis singing on the radio,
as I watched her from the window
walk across the campus –
a young robin hopping into flight –
and I sang that song to her
as we winged through ballroom skies
down tree-lined dreams.

"When I fall in love, it will be forever..."

We were young. Had not flown enough?
What did we know?

But I remember her, as I hope
she never forgot herself –
smooth as a silky thrush,
light and delicate, quivering to the touch,
and how our love with the
morning passion of the sun
laid us coupled to the ground
my holding her as I might hold and kiss
the sweet demure of a wanting bird –

or down to the afternoon kitchen floor
she soft and round
cooking young full woman warmth,
her perfect fire receiving me
whose clumsy wings
could not hold her carefully enough...

O! to be as old as we were young,
still to know and honor what we were,
and how out of our virgin passion,

children fluttered full of life and love,
and how that love, our love,
in them, through them,
loves on, flies on…

yes,
it is possible,
it might be forever.

Love Is

a terrible thing,

monstrous in its joy,
ravager of reason,
fatted up with pleasure,
all scaly ten years later.

Love is a down and out bum,
a roll over take me I'm clover,
I'm green grass, I'm soft sand,
I'm going down, down, down, down.

Love is a giant Easy with wings,
bigger than big enough to understand,
greater than needing return on its Give,
a gentle servant to the simplest kind,
to the nothing heart, the broken try.

Oh, to have understood love's terror,
its redeeming gift, its innocence,
its power, fragility, and grace, when
I had the pleasure of loving you.

Father of the West

He laid his child down,
raised a knife,
because he loved,
loved his god.

He gave his only son,
hung upon a cross,
because he loved,
loved his children.

He left a blistered handprint
to teach a lesson,
because he loved,
loved his son.

He made it for her,
made a certain place,
because he loved,
loved his wife.

He worked hard every day,
was hard how hard he worked,
because he loved,
loved his work.

His name was Mr. Grim,
the Father of the West;
it was the struggle
made him so.

He entered woman,
she needed him,

as did the children,
he needed them,

became the conqueror of space,
the keeper of the place,
would have to fight,
to keep it right,

while in his heart
he bled, an unseen red,
the texture of the thick,
thick tears he knew not how to shed.

The Keeper

He took care of her
in the abandoned house
when she was sick,
covered her with rags on that moon-down floor.

Then she left him
for the bag-man,
went to Mexico,
left him with what else came through the door:

as came the Midnight Leprechaun,
from out beneath the bushes,
and good
at making cardboard shoes;

and came the Captain of the Spoons,
who sailed a hurricane
of babbling seas,
turbulent and wild;

and came the tear-dropped Mimi,
bleary-eyed with green-striped hair
and no way home,
whose "Daddy did me dirty! Don't look at Mimi that way!"

and came the Scavengers
of dog-time alleyways,
bone-tired
from trash-can and Dumpster days.

And more there were
who landed on that hard-luck floor,
he took care of
until someone called the agencies.

But he'd been the keeper of
the abandoned house,
(which they tore down)
and he'd kept it with love
through all their cold dreams.

Ode to my Wallet

It's hard
to let go
an old wallet,
which has a thousand times
defended me,
affirming who I am –

its black leather pockets
soft and cool in my hand,
flipped open
like the wings of a bird –

to fly me safely
through the guarded gates,
steel bank doors,
sirened, mid-night, cold-road stops
by cops,

or carry me
to food and drink, work and fun
(and to that extra measure
of love that comes to one
with a nicely feathered wallet).

Countless times a day I've patted it
to reaffirm its presence.
And if it were not there,
with panicked heart,
I could not go on
until it had been found.

But it can't do it anymore.

And to this faithful bundle –
now loose at the seams,
threads come undone,

taped here and there,
floppingly empty,

its wings
unfeathered –

I must say,
goodbye.

In the Turning of Leaves

Hers was the smell
of springtime to me
sweaty perfumed Spring

tangled up in awkward yearning
kisses hot like matches burning
bright sunny bird-singing daze
walking the fields home from her house
her frilly white blouse

when we were sixteen.

Fifty springs later, fifty snows down
she an old woman bent over the counter

I sat down beside her remembering spring
(how can we have it again and again?)
sat there beside her, gray-haired and wrinkly;
smelled the dusky aroma of age,

and wondered about the changes in me
earth in the autumn, moments like these
pleasures remembered preparing to seed

walking the fields home from her house
her frilly white blouse, me on the wing –

now in the turning of leaves…

Lost in the Woods

We came so close.
We walked within a couple feet of her.
She could not hear.
She was dying from a hunger for love,
almost dead from thirst for love.
She could not hear our call, or,
what she heard, could not believe.

She went, I think, to a kiss
on the other side of sleep.

Finding Today

Inside the winter morning
in bed with yesterday
waking with regret

must find today

not to remember
not to forget

must find today

drive up the coast
out of the redwoods
the moist dark halls
shafts of sunlight
shining through

out to the ragged
winter greenings
along the river bank
the river running brown
with yesterday's rain
and washed-off earth

at the river's end
the ocean muddied
with yesterday's loss
carried now to the bathing sea

I stop beside the road
stand above a cove

below
on the belly of the beach
a belt of soft white foam
the lazy rolling waves

and if you were here with me
and I brushed back your thick rich hair
the light from your face
the glow of your beauty...

down below

a creek
floods out between cypress trees
around rocks
across the sandy beach
delivering
to the sea

the pure rush of you
the bubbling brook of your love
washing over me
caressing and kissing me
your body pressed into me
by the surging flowing current of your love

you twirl away
turning
sighing
whirling back
into my arms

you
exquisite and clear
there here
in the memory of my arms...

then
up from the beach below
a gull appears
floats almost to the road
sweeps back along the cliffs

a light easy breeze
cools my face
the fresh moist air

> *and you*
> *walk to me*
> *I look to see you*
> *all spangles and scarves*
> *twirlings and skirts*
> *dazzled and blinded*
> *I can't really see*
> *but then*
> *you come close*
> *and*
> *sunlight and peaches*
> *daisies and dew drops*
> *creamy and honey*
> *purring and touching*
> *and silence*
> *and sighs*
> *and I float like a swan*
> *into your eyes...*

become the water
the water under the bridge
gone

I drive on
past the love bloomed
the flower undone
returned to the ground

the lush wet earth
washed out to sea

drive on
and I cruise

past jack pines cypress sunlight
I breathe the smell of sheep's wet wool
pastures sloping to the sea

on
in to
today

find a friend
visit her home
eat some bread
drink some tea
walk down the trail
to the ocean beach

the setting sun
with golden light
makes of the driftwood
golden sticks

makes golden rocks
a golden stream
golden cliffs
golden sand beneath my feet

and then the sun is down
below the gold and blue marbled sky
the cool sandstone earth
and now the gleaming bowl of a moon

out at sea
on the horizon
the glimmering light of a
solitary fishing boat

down the coast
the rolling surf
silhouetted rocks

fading cliffs
misty hills
yesterday
today
ages

the distances that came between us
the distances we could not cross
nor did we need to
you will be all right and so will I

I breathe in the fresh sea air
walk up the path through lavender light

sleep in a house that hangs on a cliff
a cliff slipping inch by inch
until it tumbles too
like yesterday did
into the shimmering sea.

Old Friends

Good old friendships
have a sacredness about them,

a reverence for something greater
than perfection.

I've heard Jesus
will forgive us all –

all us good old friends,
who let each other down,
do each other wrong,
forget to pay our dues,
give each other plenty cause
to sing the doggoned blues –

heard that Jesus would
forgive us all,
if we just ask,
maybe so,
seems hard to know.

But one thing's sure to me:
as certain as one has a good old friend,
there's been forgiveness there, and –

though
that forgiveness
calls not for adoration,
no need to kneel and pray,
it happens every day,
is more or less just so,
and is most often left unsaid –

it is a sacred bloody gift,
and all of heaven I need to know.

Waiting

Like an ancient marble sculpture
carved out of a mountain,
her head resting on a pillow of clouds,
my mother lies in her bed.

We humble people – her children
her husband, nurse, friends –
approach quietly and look up at her.

Great peace radiates from her aged face.
Eyes closed, but seeing beyond our worried strife,
she waits,
quietly she waits…

We try not to disturb her.
What can we say that matters?
I love you, Mother.
I want to tell you a thousand times
I love you.

She nods and whispers,
I love you.

Me? this little snot of a boy?
this little brat?
I heard her say it,
yes, and it
makes me feel okay.

At the foot of the mountain
I reach out to touch her,
to rub her feet,
and to stay awhile with her to wait…

River Flowing Far Beyond

Swallows sweep the river in their flight.
Lilies close their petals to the night.
River flowing far beyond
Gently carry my mother on.

Here now with the setting of the sun,
Here between what was and what's to come,
River flowing far beyond
Gently carry my mother on.

Ah, how quiet is the evening light.
Bring her to the goodness of the night.
River flowing far beyond
Gently carry my mother on.

love

Made in the USA
Middletown, DE
06 May 2022

65341000R00040